The Good Snooze Guide of Great Britain

by
Robin Bennett

Illustrations *by* Jude Bennett

The Good Snooze Guide of Great Britain (Monster Books Ltd).

Originally published in Great Britain by Monster Books, The Old Smithy, Henley-on-Thames, Oxon. RG9 2AR. Published in November 2024.

All rights reserved. No part of this publication may be reproduced or transmitted in any form or by any means, electronic or mechanical, including photo-copying, recording or any information storage retrieval system, without prior permission in writing from the publishers.

The right of Robin Bennett to be identified as author of this work has been asserted by him in accordance with the Copyright, Designs and Patents Act 1988.

Text copyright Robin Bennett.
Illustration copyright Jude Bennett.

This book is sold subject to the condition that it shall not, by way of trade or otherwise, be lent, resold, hired out or otherwise circulated without the publisher's prior consent in any form of binding or cover other than that in which it is published and without a similar condition including this condition being imposed on the subsequent purchaser.

Hardback ISBN   9798338508756

A catalogue record of this book is available from the British Library.

Typesetting/layout
medievalbookshop.co.uk

This book is dedicated to indolence in all its forms.

Introduction

*To die, to sleep –
To sleep, perchance to dream – ay there's the rub.
For in that sleep of death what dreams may come...*

W. Shakespeare, *Hamlet*

I don't like sleeping: there, I've said it.

That's to say, deep sleep – the level of unconsciousness that feels like you've just spent several hours in a coma – has always struck me as the slumber equivalent of people who go to those all-you-can-eat buffet diners you drive past on the outskirts of small cities. It's sleeping for quantity over quality.

Closing my eyes and effectively cancelling myself from the world for nearly half of a whole day is like falling into a cheerless abyss. And I'll have to somehow crawl myself out of it, painfully, several hours later when the alarm goes off or my bladder is about to do me some terrible injury.

Whilst I gorged myself on Oblivion.

Like love, sleep is something to savour but perhaps never lose yourself to. Discovering, in my youth, that I had a knack for dropping off almost anywhere, at will, then waking fully-refreshed and with a slightly-altered perspective around twenty-three minutes later was fortuitous.

And quite practical: by all appearances, I have packed in quite a lot in my first half century, so I don't believe siestas have harmed me as a productive member of society.

It cut my nighttimes to around six hours and early morning starts weren't a problem. In fact, they were perfect as I had an excuse to get places I needed to be for work ahead of time and wander about until I drifted off for forty winks somewhere pleasant and of my choosing.

Over the years of doing this and that, some of the very best of times have been spent in that half-world of haze. It's repose with a consciousness of the world around me, through a pleasant filter.

This small tome is a celebration of taking it easy, of loafing about but it's also a chance for me to write about some of my favourite places and an excuse to visit new ones I like the sound of.

It's a guidebook – *for lazy people*.

Always nap when you can. It is cheap medicine.
Lord Byron

Place
The Wittenham Clumps.

Yes, but where, exactly?
Atop two perfect hills in South Oxfordshire that gaze down on English history: the eye travels through the centuries from the Iron Age – westerly, to the Age of the Iron (and other electrical items) that is Didcot – easterly.

Time of day
Just gone 3 ... or cosying betwixt the Dark Ages and the eventual Dawn of England.

Conditions
Blustery but agreeably warm for late October.

Drifting off pleasantly
Tricky, it was busier than expected.

Assisted by
Stout walk up a steep hill.

Dreams?
Not as such.

Revelations?
In a half-conscious state, wind combing dry grass sounds like the ocean.

Upon waking
Stretched back, which went off with a pleasant click, then lay there watching galleon clouds traverse an almost-infinite sea of sky.

Overall rating
Tip top, thanks.

FIELDNOTES

Like all great loves, I first admired the 'Clumps' from afar. Throughout the Seventies, it was usually as my father drove his Hillman Imp (recklessly) from Reading to Oxford with us clinging on in mortal fear at the back. In the Eighties, I would pass them on infrequent pilgrimages to see aged relatives. By the Nineties, I'd almost clean forgotten their existence until I came across them again, having quit London for a simpler life.

Volcanic cones, softened by time, sprouting grass and grazing sheep, they are the sort of hills that whisper *climb me, and you'll somehow be a better person for it.*

I parked at a jaunty angle by the Saxon Church St Cuthberts[1], this quaint cornerstone of Little Wittenham Village and the gateway to Days Lock, the Thames and then the great world beyond. This is the Clumps' equivalent of the North Face of the Eiger – it's an authentic slog to the top but, once your tunnelling vision clears and your heart rate dips out of the red, it bestows the best view.

It feels like heartlands, but this was once a frontier.

---

[1] He of Lindisfarne fame – see later.

There are the corrugated Roman earthworks, mitigated by grass, the post-card church, the silver ribbon of the Thames and all Oxfordshire laid out where there was once the southern extent of the Polar Ice Sheet.

And, talking of ice sheets, the rather nice 18th century house next to the church used to be the home of Apsley Cherry-Garrard, author of *The Worst Journey in the World*. He knew a thing or two about ice, specifically, and sleep, in general, did our Apsley. In fact, a man who knew more about what the elements could throw at you and how that can spoil a good kip would be harder to find.

In spite of having no polar experience, Cherry-Garrard managed to get himself invited by Scott to go out to Antarctica with him, purely on the basis – it seems – of being a 'good egg'. And Scott, that great leader of men, was right: Apsley proved to be such a stalwart, he was allowed to accompany Edward Wilson and Henry Bowers on a trip to collect Emperor Penguin Eggs some hundred and ninety miles away.

During the Polar Winter.

That is to say, in the perpetual dark, through a constant howling gale and temperatures around minus fifty. Given their equipment, knowledge of what they were in for and timing, it's essentially the hardest physical thing I think you could dream up doing on Planet Earth.

And it was all in the name of Science – Recapitulation Theory – the idea that studying embryos could unlock how species have developed. In this case, birds.

Sleep for them was a kind of torture on top of the very real torture of dragging three hundred kilos of frozen gear on runners that wouldn't slide because it was too cold to create the melted layer needed between metal and ice. It was probably a lot like dragging a very large wardrobe across rubble in the frozen dark. However, the team leader, Wilson, turned out to be a big believer in sleep, which meant he insisted they pitch their tent at strict six-hour intervals in order to get into frozen sleeping bags, then lie there and listen to the howling wind. And sing hymns to keep their spirits up: a robustly Edwardian and somehow quite moving detail.

Unsurprisingly sleep, invariably, wouldn't come. This wasn't helped by the fact that everything they had to keep warm had taken on a sort of perma-frost version of itself, so their underclothes, furs and bedding might as well have been made of slabs of concrete for all the good it did them.

And then their tent blew away.

This is one of those *Degrees of Funny-cum-Calamity* events: a tent flying off in a high wind is hilarious in Carry On films; slightly-less-so-but-we-laughed-about-it-later whilst camping in North Wales. But for them it was a life or death turn of events. And they would have all died but for the fact that, by some miracle, it snagged on a rock and they somehow managed to find it in the almost total darkness and screeching tempest.

In spite of losing their tent, a lot of teeth and very nearly all their fingers and toes, they very occasionally got some rest and also managed to pinch an egg from what must have been a terrifically flabbergasted penguin had it known the lengths some humans had gone to, seemingly to make an omelette. It was a triumph snatched from the jaws of foolhardiness.

Alas, having finally got the egg back to England, The British Museum was non-plussed to say the least, even going as far to claim to never have received it twelve months later, before coming to the conclusion that Emperor Penguin eggs weren't of much scientific interest.

The resulting book, *The Worst Journey in the World* is, though: the journey itself, not the goal and Apsley's account became the justification. It's truly gripping, if only as one of the most modest accounts of naïvety, good humour and stunning bravery peculiar to a certain type of Englishman.

Thoughts of great, long journeys, the walk up here and an Indian Summer sun brought me to the conclusion I shouldn't be over-taxing myself. I should rest.

Considering it was Monday, the Clumps were abnormally busy. I sat on a bench with a decent view of Days Lock, only to be immediately joined by an oldish man in a bright blue anorak who popped out of nowhere. He had one of those overly lively faces that often indicate a degree of inner turmoil. I half smiled, and nodded in his direction, which only made him sigh and stare at a tree, so I decided to move on and leave him to his monologues.

A tour of the first hill felt more like a bank holiday. *Don't people have jobs*, I thought grumpily before discovering that the second hill was much quieter, partly because it was littered with small brown cows and partly because the view isn't as chocolate boxy.

Still nice, I thought as I settled myself and considered Shillingford Hill in the middle distance, with it's one tree on top and the curly fringe on the horizon that is Harpsden Woods – the oldest surviving forest in Britain, I'm told.

Sleep came by gentle degrees and soon I was aware only of the soft grass at my back, the still-warm sun and a temperate, vaguely cowy, breeze. Then, of not quite anything but peace.

Small brown cows live for small yellow apples it turns out, because I was woken by the sound of one or two of them munching noisily a few yards away.

I watched them for a bit, then closed my eyes again, so I didn't have to rush. Outdoor snoozing in the right conditions trumps sleeping on a comfortable surface indoors, which trumps an actual bed for some reason.

This was my only memorable thought as I got up slowly and found the path that led to where the car was parked and back to the real world.

November

We were all Romans once, I guess.
Omar Epps

Place
Hadrian's Wall.

Yes, but where, exactly?
Sycamore Gap, before it was massacred.

Time of day
The horizon smudged blue grey as dusk settled in on the landscape.

Conditions
Dry but you need layers and a warm dog. Or any other friendly mammal.

Drifting off pleasantly
Easy peasy.

Assisted by
Nothing but fresh air and a sense of boundless freedom.

Dreams?
Vivid scenes of recent events replayed. Awoke with a minor convulsion.

Revelations?
I always thought this wall was more symbolic. It's not. And perhaps I should start bringing one of those airline pillows on these outings.

Upon waking
Scoffed an Aero.

Overall rating
Pointy but refreshing.

FIELDNOTES

Hadrian's Wall is an elusive stone serpent. It slides behind Northumbrian hills and into Northumbrian hollows, hugging the landscape before disappearing from sight into dark, Northumbrian woodland. I have crossed its path dozens of times and only briefly spied this pagan snake of stone that separated the modern world of Pax Romana from The Chaos: the sheep stealers and hairy, angry men. The scorners of togas and totalitarianism.

Usually, by this stage of any car journey between the Home Counties and a brief holiday in Scotland, the idea of stopping the car to look at something you're not quite sure is where you expect it to be lacks appeal. This is especially so when measured against the strong possibility of a blazing fire in the hotel bar on the shores of Loch Lomond.

But today would be the day I finally got to grips with it.

I got up early, chucked the dog in the back of the car and set off; hoping the embers of the Indian summer we were having wouldn't splutter out as we ventured north.

My goal (the one right after I'd accidentally-on-purpose stopped for a MacDonald's breakfast) was the town of Brampton: achieved if you put your foot down and head straight at Carlisle, then ricochet off its suburbs, sort of North by North-east. The A69 is one of those long roads that could almost be in the USA (if the USA had farms with Viking-sounding names and the Pennines for a backdrop). It's also got the cheapest petrol station ever – somewhere between Brampton and the Roman Fort of *Vercovicium*.

This sounds like a failed brand of cough medicine but is, in point of truth, the largest surviving Roman Fort on the wall that generally had them at intervals of seven and a third miles with mini ones in between to make sure nobody common snuck across it. This wouldn't have been easy, given it was fifteen foot high in most places.

The Roman Command structure must have loved walls and the whole business of populating them with soldiers from the far-flung reaches of their empire. But, when they weren't keeping busy, they were also big on sleep, rightly feeling that you couldn't successfully carpe your busy deum of massacring the locals then dishing out law, order and conjugating, unless you'd had a good six hours rest at night and a midday snooze.[2] In fact, they're likely to have invented the siesta, the Spanish word being derived from the Latin word *hora sexta* "sixth hour" (counting from dawn, whence they retired to their couch at midday).

Or, at least, they claimed they invented it – same as they did with columns, sandals and free speech.

I parked the car in an empty carpark at the Vercovicium site (aka Housesteads Roman Fort), then had a short moral tussle with myself over whether to pay for parking out of season. To take my mind off all that guilt, I reflected that sleep must have been a boon for the legionnaires – plucked from blazing hot Mediterranean and North Africa states and plonked all the way up here to fight angry, cold people.

Unlike them, I couldn't very well warm up by asserting my superiority violently on the passing German hikers encased head to toe in man-made fibre or the elderly couple who smiled at me and said hello as they tottered past, so we set off up the hill

---

[2] Known as a 'biphasic' sleeping culture, i.e. two accepted rest periods. Same as in Medieval England, although they didn't sleep during the day, rather split the night in two, in order to drag themselves out of nice warm beds to chant and fret about when the Black Death was coming to visit.

instead, passing the Roman ruins at the virtual jog of those that have been in the car too long.

That did the trick.

Cooper (scruffy spaniel) who had the wind up his tail, forked left and dived into a thicket. There was a flurry of activity followed by the exit of an improbable pheasant that complained loudly as it flew low up the rest of the hill then loped over what was my first proper sighting of The Wall. I was warm enough by now to stop and lean against the cold stone cobbles that make up its flanks, recalibrating to the level of emptiness around these parts that never fails to take me by surprise as I assume England is going to have some sort of building everywhere you look.

Yet, seemingly endless humps of small hills abound – green then greying into the distance – ferned valleys, strewn with rocks the colour of old bone and small woodlands deployed like regimental defensive squares. And very much part of it all, by virtue of building skills and their sense of practical aesthetics, the roman wall, far from home but very much at home.

For the next sixty minutes, I walked alongside it, on it, slightly removed from it and eventually came to my destination, the familiar dip and tree where Kevin Costner made friends with Morgan Freeman back in 1991, hardly central to the Robin Hood story but that scene somehow entering into cinema history by virtue of place.

Apart from a few cows, like fluffy teddy bears, and a couple who asked to me to take their picture, there was no-one else in sight, so I got out my picnic of processed meats, crisps and popular chocolate bars, and munched away very happily, chucking bits of pork pie and cheap salami at the dog in between mouthfuls.

By and by, I finished up and made myself comfortable against the ancient wall itself and fell asleep almost immediately.

It was an intrinsically healthy siesta.

Cooper woke me with a succession of sneezes – his way of telling me he is keen to get going. But it was just as well, as dusk beckoned, I was getting cold and rocks that definitely weren't there when I fell asleep had grown out of the ground and were sticking into my kidneys. I guessed I had about thirty minutes of real light left, plus a few minutes of fringy-vestigy stuff I could count on given the expanse of sky and lack of cloud.

In the end, I had fifteen minutes of glorious sunset, then darkness and stars as I arrived back at Homestead Fort and turned downhill towards the silent visitor centre and my lonely car.

I was off to Durham next stop, where my hotel was ... and beer.

December

Libraries are where it all begins.
Rita Dove

Place
Royal Holloway (London University).

Yes, but where, exactly?
Founder's Library, where it all began.

Time of day
Twilight on a winter's day.

Conditions
Bookish.

Drifting off pleasantly
After a fashion.

Assisted by
The soporific effect of classic lit.

Dreams?
Hardly got a chance.

Revelations?
Hell is indeed other people - usually much younger ones.

Upon waking
Glared about angrily.

Overall rating
Meh ...

FIELDNOTES

If there was one *femme fatale* amongst the girls I went to university with, it had to be Rebecca.

Rebecca was a couple of years younger than me, but I used to sit with her when I went to screenings of art nouveau cinema or anything else a bit pretentious that none of my actual friends would be seen dead at. She'd already had articles published in a few national broadsheets, and she looked like Kate Beckinsale did around about the same time. But better.

I thought that was pretty cool, but mostly I was content that she was not my problem: I had just about enough sense in those days to know that Rebecca was Trouble and that it was, therefore, safest to appreciate her with a degree of detachment. I knew several people who had fallen for her and the lure of the salon she had gathered together, like interesting nick-nacks made up of mainly richer students in an exclusive and aesthetically pleasing part of the Founder's Building. And they all went about the place looking distracted and miserable, as if nothing meant anything unless they were sipping tea in her rooms, discussing Proust, whilst being treated to the sight of her perfect hands perching a book on perfect knees.

The salon-of-sorts was on the top floor and had a turret room on a split-level. There were about six studies there, and throughout my time at Royal Holloway they were always allocated to a certain type of undergrad. Had it been Harry Potter, they would all have been in Slytherin.

As I say, I used to pop up from time to time but was content I could take it or leave it.

In my final year I made myself a sort of secret den on the ground floor of the library, facing the ornate quadrangle, flanked by French Literature: *Boetie* to *Descartes* on my left; *Flaubert* to yet more *Flaubert* on my right. I went there most afternoons to daydream and read anything but the actual set course literature.

Then, one day, I came round from my habitual semi-conscious dream state to see Rebecca through the library window, tapping the pane with the curved end of a red nail. Her hair was up, which is how it looked best because you could see more of her freckle-dusted face. When she smiled, which she was doing now, her eyes crinkled and her small, neat teeth contrasted with her *pièce that would accept no resistance*. Rebecca looked and sounded like the dutiful and demure catholic girl she was for the most part. However, sometime or another her mouth had had other ideas: red lips, almost indecently full with a permanent uptick at the corners, like an amused feline. Rebecca was Bronte, her mouth was the Kama Sutra.

The sensual can so easily become the erotic by the play of light. I was half asleep, caught unawares but with the sudden suspicion, looking at her finely-lit features, that I'd been in love for a while without really knowing it.

She motioned for me to come closer. So, I did, half rising from my desk until our faces were very close either side of the window. She was smiling at me and then she half closed her eyes and those lips parted. Instinctively, I leaned in, and she did so, too.

We kissed, our lips not touching through the glass ... but that is still my kiss – my *Memento Amori*. It felt as if everything we knew about romance, everything we felt about each other went into that moment, separated by a few millimetres of clear pane.

Years later, when I read the final chapter of *One Fine Day*, the line

> ... *and they kissed in the street as all around them people hurried home in the summer light, and it was the sweetest kiss that either of them would ever know.*

made me think of that moment, as I leaned across my strewn notes and we bridged a gap though the cool glass with intention. The cleaners should have hung their heads in shame, too, for each time I looked up from my studies until the last of my finals were taken and I left, I could see that kiss, still hanging there, in Rebecca's fading lipstick.

Royal Holloway presides over Egham atop its very own small hill – as fine example of Victorian Gothic as you'll ever find or a big pinkish cake of a place, depending on your taste and mood. Four-cornered and turreted, to look like Chambord, but stoutly built out of honest Victorian bricks.

I had a sense of high expectation as I parked the car in a leafy spot by some attractive balustrade. This pilgrimage had a fair bit to live up to.

And, to begin with, things went well. By looking like I belonged, plus a bit grumpy, no-one asked what I was doing when I walked into the library. Past the modern turnstile, I went up the gently undulating parquet stairs, through the double doors with their stained-glass inserts and breathed in the Victorian library smell of books, brass, polished mahogany and dust.

Sneezing discreetly, I made my way to the end of the main

library and took a staircase to a ground floor auxiliary wing that used to house obscure periodicals, damaged books and what were considered out-moded critical works – all of no use to any god nor man except, in my case, for prevarication and loafing. And naps.

At the very end of a narrow corridor of books, where nobody used to venture, I found my old desk.

And I could not have been more pleased, absolutely nothing had changed in 30 years, so I sat down, pulled out an annotated copy of *Trois Contes*, more or less at random, and prepared to let French literature do its stuff.

Yet hardly had I closed my eyes, when I was woken with a start by the sound of several sets of feet on the stairs, bags been thrown on the floor and chairs dragged back.

'Here's good,' said a confident girl's voice and there were three or four grunts of ascension as another girl with a heavy Spanish accent asked.

'Does anyone have the notes from last time?'

My heart began to sink. Didn't undergraduates go to the pub anymore when they needed to have a group discussion? Libraries are for quiet contemplation, sexual tension and sleep.

Turned out they were business studies students and the case study they were discussing meant that every three or four minutes someone had to interrupt someone else loudly and a bit rudely with a 'Yeah, but ...' then dive off at a tangent.

This was hopeless, plus I was beginning to feel like an imposter: they couldn't see me where I was and the way they were talking indicated they thought they were alone in this forgotten rump of the library.

So I grasped the nettle of British embarrassment, grabbed my things and walked out to shocked silence of young people suddenly finding they have a middle aged eavesdropper in their midst.

Then I went home.

As excursions go, it was a re-run: it lacked authenticity and the gods of sleep had punished me.

Still, it *had* been nice to sit a while at that old desk, to think back to those early days of wool gathering and the never-repeated feeling we all try and fail to recapture, of being young and very much in love.

January

Democracy is the recurrent suspicion that more than half of the people are right more than half of the time.

E. B. White

Place
Houses of Parliament.

Yes, but where, exactly?
Visitor's Gallery.

Time of day
Right after a good lunch.

Conditions
Warm and safe, rising to troubled – almost rowdy – before subsiding to a gentle subtext.

Drifting off pleasantly
Like the well-oiled gears of governance.

Assisted by
Guile.

Dreams?
Occupied an out-of-body space. Aware of my surroundings whilst slipping from one interloping mental plane to another.

Revelations?
Unexpected fondness for democracy. Most of government and governing is safe ... but dull. Ideal conditions for forty winks.

Upon waking
Straightened up and nodded vigorously, as if I agreed with everything being said ... then walked off.

Overall rating
Perfect example of how sleep and Democracy can work together in the public sphere.

FIELDNOTES

I like London. It has more than its fair share of the tip topmost music, sports, eating, drinking, swag-making, flag-waving and park-going places on Planet Earth. Nevertheless, I prefer to look upon it with these days from a safe distance, with twinkly avuncularity. It's a young man's game.

And if I must take the train to Town, I'm going to get a good meal out of it. I like Rules near Covent Garden because it is very old, filled with the sort of pictures and furniture I wish I was allowed to have everywhere at home and it's seasonal.

I started making plans for a blow out with a good book.

Then, as is often the way, Bomber Command got wind of it and announced her intention of coming along to keep an eye on me over the claret and Armagnac.

Lunching à deux requires a different sort of vibe, so we booked The Colony Grill room in Mayfair, which is worth it just for the staircase going down to the loos.

Two thirds of a bottle of Chasse Spleen to the good (plus one gin, one pudding wine and the essential *digestif*) and I was ready for a brisk walk followed by my afternoon nap. With H happily tacking her way along Oxford Street, due course Liberty's, I made my way just as happily to the Seat of Democracy, for a seat.

I got through security, passed a trifling sort of queue and got off my sore feet just as the Right Hon Mr Tobias Ellwood (Bournemouth East) (Con) got on his and started telling us about Pokesdown Railway station.

It seems that after Bournemouth, Weymouth and even Boscombe, Pokesdown – as a destination – comes a poor fourth. Trumped by Bournemouth and Weymouth, OK ... but those dicks in Boscombe really get their goat in Pokesdown.

Clearly something had to be done, and Mr Ellwood had the answer. A spruced-up railway station. With nice lifts.

... it had been about three minutes in and, I was settling nicely. The trembling wings of sleep were already flicking at the edge of my consciousnesses, but I also found myself strangely gripped by the state of south coast railways and the fate of Pokesdown. A part of me was fretting.

However, in a further twist, it turned out that the money (couple of million quid, if you please) was already in place. The Right Hon member for Bournemouth East (Con), was only talking to us today because he wanted things to get a wiggle on.

Barring a late intervention by the Boscombe Mob to scupper the deal, I knew that all would be well.

So surrounded by the smell of polish, politics and leather, a mostly empty Gallery and the benign working of democratic government, my eyelids drooped and Mr Ellwood's voice receded like a train down an endless track of slumber.

I can't have been out for more than a few blissful minutes, when someone bumped my leg. This was premature. Fourteen minutes is the bare minimum, in my experience, for a decent nap that revives but won't affect a good night's sleep or your ability to leap up at a moment's notice and operate machinery. Over thirty-ish and I find I feel sluggish and drowsy for a good hour afterwards.

This was my fault, as I was wearing a hat indoors, pulled low, so no-one could see I was sleeping.

Looking like you're not asleep, when you patently are, requires some skill. A hat is useful but not always to hand/head. Another technique I have developed over the years I dub *Le Penseur*. You lean forward, elbows on knees, hands shielding eyes as if deep in thought. Or prayer. Works well in church and AA meetings. Some lucky souls can manage forty winks standing up. I call this *Le Militaire* as career soldiers are usually quite good at it. Helps if you have a handy wall or tree that hasn't been bombed flat, but true artists tell me that by placing your feet around 40 cm apart means you can get some kip and not topple over whilst guarding the Realm against its mortal enemies. The key is having your weight evenly-spaced and relaxing your core, I gather.

Thanks to the double Armagnac and gallons of fresh air, I didn't have long to feel short-changed, as I almost immediately drifted off again into what can be described as a *deep daydream*. I stretched my legs out to discourage the casual wanderer and let myself soak in the woody atmosphere in this waking reverie.

Pugin's parliament was built at a time when I suppose we were at our most self-confident as a nation – rather suddenly finding ourselves running the largest empire in history. Almost by chance. That is to say, there had been no Grand Plan to control nearly a quarter of the world population and about the same percentage of total land area, no Causus Belli or religious fervour driving us on. There was just a vague feeling that it all seemed to be working on a practical level and so we might as well keep plugging away at it.

Whilst no empire is inherently good – or in perpetuity – at least some of what has remained *could* be described as OK: a global lingua franca with lots of lovely words but easy peasy grammar, a mass roll out of democracy and the three most popular sports in the world (Football, Rugby and Cricket).

And this eye-catching building: grand but granular in its detail – especially the Lord's which is decorated inch by inch without coming across as gaudy. Many great public buildings look good on postcards but, close up, in all their austere bulkiness, seem to be simply making one point only: we're really big. Behave.

Other parliament chambers when I see them on TV, resemble school theatres. They are often soulless echoey places with squeaky plastic chairs and very bright lights.

I was recently invited to visit the House of Lords. By a Lord. Michael Jay (Baron[3] of Ewelme) gave me the full tour and then a full cup of tea.

Over which he explained that one of the major benefits of the Houses of Parliament is that, in spite of the fact a lot of it might be slowly crumbling towards the Thames, it is still very practical – being virtually the only democratic building on the planet where both houses sat cheek by jowl and all business can be conducted, or conduited, by simply popping across the hall.

The Minister of State, Department for Transport (Huw Merriman) was now assuring Mr Ellwood in what was an incredibly round about manner that things were in hand, and so the Commons very much seemed to be wrapping up for the day.

I stole a glance at my watch and saw it was high time to meet H at Paddington. Gave a tremendous stretch, which it suddenly occurred to me looked a bit like I was sticking my hand up in class, so yanked my arm down before anyone asked me if I needed the loo.

I retired from the Public Gallery, wondering, as I made my way towards St Stephen's entrance[4], if I hadn't missed my

---

[3] The title of 'Baron' ranks slightly higher than that of a common or garden Lord. In simplified terms, it goes: Emperor/Empress, then King/Queen, Grand Duke/Grand Duchess, Prince/Princess, Duke/Duchess, Marquess/Marchioness, Earl/Countess, Viscount/Viscountess, Baron/Baroness, Lord/Lady, Sir/Lady ... Pleb/Pleb's Missus.

[4] Via St Stephen's Hall, which people seem to forget was the site of original House of Commons from the mid 16th century. This was also where Richard, Duke of York – and one of the poor Princes in the Tower – was married to Ann Mowbray. She was older than him (aged five to his four years). In further news, the suffragette, Emily Davison spent the night in the broom cupboard here, intending to jump out and address the House of Commons on women's rights the next day. Tony Benn, MP put up a plaque in the closet to commemorate the event. I hope he polished it.

calling: it takes one to know one, meaning quite a few MPs also appeared to be nodding off.

And they had comfier benches.

February

Sleep is the best meditation.
Dalai Lama

Place
Milton Keynes.

Yes, but where, exactly?
A private flotation tank.

Time of day
Decent interval before tea.

Conditions
More Space Age than New Age. And dark ... oh, so very dark.

Drifting off pleasantly
For want of other distractions, yes.

Assisted by
Getting over the fear of drowning.

Dreams?
Just for a world made of rainbows and love.

Revelations?
With self-awareness comes the power to cut through the chains of self-doubt and become beautiful beings of light ... obvs.

Upon waking
Vigorous shower.

Overall rating
Zen.

FIELDNOTES

In an unassuming cul-de-sac that defines the general unremarkableness of Milton Keynes suburbia, there's a low rise building devoted to Wellness.

It hosts a mini-Spa advertising massages plus 'treatments' and a place you can pay good money to go dark orange or reddish brown, depending on your taste and or undercoat. Then there's a purveyor of Flotation Tank experiences, run by a guy called Bob.

Not really.

The man who buzzed me in, introduced himself as Richard and had a reassuringly blokey demeanour – more chilled gym coach than guru.

I filled in a form, which – apart from the usual checks I wasn't at death's door – asked me not to do anything in the tank I wouldn't do in front of my own grandmother (except get naked, I hoped). I was then given a menu of the music I wanted to be played whilst in the tank. Nothing with whales thankfully and, in the absence of a tick box for Norwegian Death Metal – for the challenge, I went for the gentle sound of waves breaking against a shoreline – for the relevance. Then hoped it wasn't overkill.

Bob/Richard came back from somewhere that was a bit of a mystery. Given the fact the reception area and pre-chillout room were essentially the same room, I assumed he must have been hiding in a cupboard for the last ten minutes.

He grabbed my form off me, gave it a quick scan and commended my choice of music, like a waiter agreeing with one's choice of wine. Then he led me into The Tank Room.

I think I'd been expecting something that looked like a tube people sit in for MRI scans or use for going on very long space journeys in movies. This essentially looked like it was designed by someone who was thinking, at the time, about giant Smarties.

Bob/Richard also seemed inclined to hang about and chat. He pointed out the shower, the towels and – massively unnecessarily – the giant tank. Then he asked me what I did for a living, so I told him I was in IT, to get him to go away.

Which he did.

And, so, I soon found myself sliding into the Dead Sea salt water and shutting the door to the world.

I'd barely gathered the very few thoughts habitually in my head before I drifted off into a profound slumber I'm going to dub *Mega Napping*. Total absconsion for a brief interval – like God has hit you on the head with a celestial brick. Five minutes, tops, I'm guessing but I successfully blanked out the splashy shoreline sounds from the musical soundtrack to my 'experience' and the more real splashy sounds of the giant bath I was in. This was a Void.

Then I woke.

Like I'd been tasered because I suddenly remembered I'm scared of the dark (it was very dark) and at least two thirds of my head was underwater.

I scrabbled about for a few unnerving moments before I found the light switch to my 'pod' and breathed a very real sigh of relief that always washes over me when I can see what's going on.

I bobbed about for a bit under a mauve light, marvelling at how half a ton of salt in warm water essentially produces a liquid mattress. I've never been able to float successfully on my back, so this was novel enough as experiences go to use up the next five minutes whilst I practised float techniques hitherto unavailable to me (Snow Angel, King Tut … Orphelia).

At this point I remembered I that I was there in order to confront by my inner self, stripped of its worldly ambition; my mind traversing the Infinite Continuum, seemingly at random, yet perhaps just Destination Unknowable as it floated on infinite waves, served up by the universe, ISOPod© and AI music. And that I wasn't there just to splash about.

Prior to this visit, I had been researching meditation techniques I planned to gain complete mastery of in my allotted time. It's all a bit baffling for someone normal, but I managed to boil them down to mindfulness, mantra, muscle, breathing, transcendental and loving kindness.

Loving Kindness, (AKA LKM, or Metta), seemed a good one to practice when you're on your own in an isolation tank, as there's very little chance some idiot will come along and piss you off right in the middle of you cultivating an attitude of universal friendliness.

I imagined I was facing a loved one, concentrating all my feelings of goodwill and affection on them. For the purpose of the exercise, I chose Cooper. Choosing the dog was in no way an attempt to trivialise the issue a) I love my dog, b) choosing one of the children would be favouritism and annoy the other two – therefore limiting my chances of moving from Metta (loving kindness) to the next stage of Mudita (appreciative joy) and c) choosing my wife was a bad idea as she hates being stared at.

'May I be well, happy, and peaceful.' I mantra'd, ignoring the watery echo.

'May you be well, happy, and peaceful.' I continued, concentrating on sending love out.

In my mind's eye the dog looked at me and wagged his tail. Cool. I didn't quite feel like I was bathing in a light of warmth, peace and loving kindness, as I was led to expect, but I definitely felt a lot more positive generally.

I repeated the mantra several times, whilst focussing on my breathing, Cooper's whole being blurred, until it was just two chocolate brown eyes looking into mine and I began to drift off again.

Whether to describe the next stage of my wellness experience as deep meditation or a gentle snooze is open to interpretation.

By and by, the sound of waves folding onto some distant shore slipped back into my consciousness, possibly because Bob/Richard turned the volume up and I felt I was nearing the end of my spiritual journey.

Although not quite.

After a leisurely shower, I was led into an even smaller room off reception and given a herbal tea and an introduction to a fellow Podee called Barbara, a nice lady who ran the yoga classes next door.

We chatted about the benefits of flotation tanks whilst I concentrated on sending positive LKM vibes her way, which completely worked as she gave me her shortbread slice.

Then Bob/Richard came in and I realised it really was over when he produced a credit card machine and asked if I minded putting a review on TrustPilot. We were back in the world of cold commercialism.

On the drive home I didn't shout at a single cyclist.

Result.

March

Ain't much for pushing buttons, pulling puppet strings or fussing,
Besides making silly rhymes I really ain't much good at nothing,
But my heart keeps me amused in this big world of confusion,
Cause I'm a dreamer,
Hallelujah I'm a dreamer..

David Egan, sung and performed
by Amy LaVere and Will Sexton

Place
Snowdonia.

Yes, but where, exactly?
The Llanberis to Mount Snowdon Railway.

Time of day
Elevenses.

Conditions
Squally to thoroughly inclement.

Drifting off pleasantly
And some.

Assisted by
Blessed warmth.

Dreams?
Rolodex of events: non sequiturs, snippets and snapshots that I guess made sense at the time.

Revelations?
Trains bend reality.

Upon waking
Stretched my legs in the silvery late March sun, considered some patches of snow.

Overall rating
Quality mid-morning kip.

FIELDNOTES

Too tight to spring for a hotel, I got up at 5am and went to the top of Wales (longitudinally) by car, in order to get to the top of Wales (topographically) by train.

This flagrant misuse of fossil fuels, even in the cause of great literature, would have to be paid penance, so I decided to forgo a cooked breakfast on the M40 by eating an apple, then a banana *en le hoof*. Lunch somewhere warm and pub-like (a pub) would also be forwent by dint of bringing a humble picnic. I stole Hélène's thermos, to feel more like Alan Bennett.

Morning forty winks was not something I ever attempted throughout my young adulthood but I came to it, as a practical necessity, when we had babies that woke up at 3am and stayed awake until five. It was then that I developed a taste for dropping off in front of reruns of *Dog the Bounty Hunter* at around 11.30am or *Murder She Wrote* on obscure satellite channels before all hell broke loose again.

As I slung shot around Birmingham, I wondered why I was going all this way – there are plenty of trains near us: even a steam train next to Didcot. Then, again, I've always wanted to visit Snowdonia. Or revisit, as we went on a school trip when I was about nine or ten. All I remember of that excursion is drinking water from a stream and listening to ELO, *Discovery* over and over, on someone's portable Panasonic cassette player at the back of the coach.

So I was going back to get some real memories.

Time slows beyond Chester. Wizened timber and wattle, it's English to its bootstraps. But the red sandstone denotes border shenanigans in my experience and soon enough I was in Arthur's country, skirting Anglesey – Ynys Môn – where the druids, taking their final refuge from the Romans, were cornered and massacred. The last tangible thread of wisdom as old as the hills I was heading for was severed, their sacred oaks cut down ... and the roots of British Magic withered.

What remains is intangible, just the feeling of something elemental and essential woven into the sinew of the landscape. And this impression grows as the hills rise, the sky becomes huge, and the horizon widens beyond your peripheral vision.

Yr Wyddfa – Mount Snowdon – looks like a child's drawing of a mountain from a distance: slopes at a perfect 45-degree pitch form a pleasing triangle with a clear summit and something to aim at.

'Would you like to download our app?'

'Um, not really. Can you explain again about the steam train?'

'It's not running until June.'

'And going to the top?'

'Our diesel train takes you about three quarters of the way up. You can walk the rest of the way and you save twenty quid on the summer prices. But we have to tell customers there are no facilities at Clogwyn Station.'

'Best go here, then.'

'I would, there aren't any trees to hide behind up there.'

'When's the next train?'

'The *first* train,' the student in the ticket office corrects me, 'is at 9am, so you've got twenty minutes.'

'Time for a coffee,' I say. 'And I can download the app.'

'I wouldn't bother,' she says.

Llanberis Station is exactly how it should be: neat and wooden, overall. Flower-bedded, green-painted, gift-shopped and café'd, to drill down to the details. There's even a small film theatre that I swerved. Although it's pleasantly in-keeping and (best of all) free, I exercised my right to experience the trip to the summit without the aid of drone footage and a voice over commentary.

I opted instead for a small guidebook and a modest cup of tea. The guide – not the tea leaves – informed me that the return journey takes two hours (allowing for a 30 minute stop over) and that the railway I was soon to be enjoying was started in 1894 and finished in 1896 (two years, which is, coincidently, the same time as it takes to get here by coach from London).

The train track I was about to enjoy from the lofty height of my comfortable train carriage was constructed with a saw tooth, stopping it slipping backwards down the steep gradient. For extra confidence and painstaking attention to detail, it was apparently invented by a Swiss gentleman.

I looked up as my eye caught movement on an up-until-now vacant platform.

9am on a weekday, outside of the holidays is decidedly off peak when it comes to your average tourist train. Add North Wales on a blustery day and be a lone male, without a socially-reassuring dog in tow, and you'll find yourself basking in isolation in your own quadrant of the single carriage on offer.

My only companions had a distinctly local look, not dressed at all like tourists, and slightly bored, as if taking the trip up once a year was a civic duty. I felt a foreigner, almost.

Leaving Oxfordshire that morning seemed like something that had happened in another era. I pressed my forehead against the glass of the carriage window, watching the station slip away.

I let my mind freewheel ... *remembering getting up, shivering, coffee, then slipping out of the house. The damp dawn air had made me cough as I shambled down the road, found the car and tipped myself in. I hit the ignition, pressed a few buttons for warmth and noise, and the next thing I remembered with any clarity was the M40 somewhere near Banbury as the crow flies.*

On the train, my compartment warmed, my eyelids drooped.

As I dozed, I was back on the road. The sound of the steel tracks in The Real merged with the memory of rubber on tarmac. *Cars switched places, in my mind's eye, faded ahead or behind.* I relived songs, snippets of same news and the narrow, cranking gauge rocked me deeper to a mind space where time folded in on itself and events that could have been today, last week, a year ago – or never – fell into logical step.

Life makes a great deal more sense during and shortly after a good snooze and this one was top drawer.

Five minutes after waking, I could no longer recall the rhyme or the reason of what I had half-dreamed or why it was relevant, but I felt tremendously rested and of the opinion that sleeping on a train is as good as it gets.

Another advantage of drifting off for the journey up, was that the view was a very agreeable revelation upon awaking. No slow unfolding of a landscape that got higher by degrees. I stepped out of Clogwyn Station and got the whole of North Wales in yer face. I would have got a bit of Ireland, too, according to my guidebook, but the weather was still untrustworthy. That said, the clouds did part, after a fashion, enough to let some ambient light grace the hills and the water in the distance that took on wrinkles, like the surface of an orange.

From above, Mount Snowden forms a circus, looking for all the world like half of it was blown to smithereens in the very distant past. This may well have been the case.

Thanks to my midmorning forty winks, I felt fantastic. Not so fantastic that I could make the return journey to the summit in the short time allowed, but good enough to walk with fierce determination uphill for fifteen minutes and bound down again, in time to catch the train back to Llanberis.

Re-seated, I was able to take it all in slowly this time: the shifting vistas of crag and slope, as we dropped back down into the valley. A couple even smiled at me as we got on, now we were fellow travellers.

Recalling a place, I've learned, is as much committing to memory how it made you feel as what you saw.

April

Here we are all, by day; by night we're hurl'd
By dreams, each one into a several world..

Robert Herrick

Place
Dunwich.

Yes, but where, exactly?
Amidst the ruins of Greyfriars Monastery.

Time
Close to twilight.

Conditions
Somewhat eerie.

Drifting off pleasantly
... to the sound of wind in the trees, both real and spectral.

Assisted by
A sense of the paranormal.

Dreams?
Visions, more like.

Revelations?
Not sure I want to go there.

Upon waking
Legged it.

Overall rating
Intense.

FIELDNOTES

Dreams are the trapdoor to tunnels that take one to realities by the horde – both comforting and unsettling. The once were, and never was. Sleep is often the small death, it is deficit.

Coming to this place on a dreary day in April feels like a summons: a subpoena to make a call on the dead. For Dunwich is also loss.

Lost land, lost lives.

More of it now lies under a grey slab of water than doesn't. And the sickle moon of what remains of the town awaits the inevitable cold maw of the North Sea, to join Doggerland – a whole kingdom drowned long since.

The carcass of All Saints Church has been dragged inland, away from its precipice. Trudging up the hill, all that remains is a solitary grave sat in a tangle of uninviting scrub.

My tramping took me to the ruins of Greyfriars Monastery. Biphasic, too, the monks would be going to bed about now – as the world went dim – rising in the small hours to chant to cross and candle in the cold gloom.

The wind had claws up here, but I stuck to my task, wrapping my coat tight and wedging myself against a wall that jutted out of the ground like a broken tooth.

I closed my eyes, breathed deeply a few times ... then fell.

The monastery had neighboured a salt marsh.

It was the same hour as in the real, as clouds trolled across the landscape. Impatient shadows crowded my peripheral vision, comfortless grey palls, shrouded and, in my sleep, I knew I'd made a mistake. But nightmares have to be seen through. They are the risk we take when we close our eyes and let our guard down.

The inner eye, the optic dreams give us when ours are closed, saw nothing but wind-blasted bleakness. A steady stream of ripples shuddered from one end of the hightide marsh to the other and made the black-ended reeds on the far shore topple to and fro. The cold gusts up here in the ruins lent my dream a bitter squall that set up a low keening sound, like the cry of a child, as a lone figure appeared from under the trees to stand by the water's edge.

The figure seemed young, head bent, making no sound whilst the wind whipped at her dress as she tiptoed closer to the water's edge. Too close. The longer she stood on the drenched shoreline, the darker it became; an unearthly murk, that crept up on the lonely figure from the clammy marshes and gathered at her thin shoulders. Though she held herself perfectly still, I sensed she was terrified.

More night than day now, in my dream, the wind took strength from this, notching from a whine to whistle. The girl advanced a step and let her shawl drop. She stood, a bent figure, with her feet in the water and her shoulders shaking. I remembered, later, that was crying.

By the time she had moved forward again, the wind was an almost human shriek, running from one side of the desolate lake to the other.

Then she simply slipped below the surface.

Moments before she disappeared from view, the girl turned her head. Her face was white against the dark background of the sky, and she stared directly at me.

Coming out of a dream like that can only go one way. Waking is to rise again.

I ran. Like Jesus probably did from the tomb.

May

*Believe me, my young friend, there is nothing—
absolutely nothing—
half so much worth doing as simply messing about in boats.*

Water Rat/Kenneth Graham, *Wind in the Willows*

Place
River Thames.

Yes, but where, exactly?
Hennerton Backwater.

Time of day
Teatime.

Conditions
Lethargic.

Drifting off pleasantly
Compared to Dunwich, absolutely.

Assisted by
Awe-inspiring propensity for idleness.

Dreams?
Of childhood and literature.

Revelations?
Ratty was quite right.

Upon waking
Drifted home peacefully.

Overall rating
Sick, bruv.

FIELDNOTES

There's a tranquil back water along the Thames between Henley and Shiplake. Well-heeled riparian folk, in characterful Edwardian houses, keep a discreet distance from the bank, each other, and the raucous turmoil that is the rest of the world.

Rivers – small ones especially – have the ability to slow life down agreeably. Hennerton Backwater more than most. To navigate along this brief digression from the Thames is to dial back the years from present day to a less frenetic sometime in 1909.

Decades ago, I remember it choked with debris: a flotsam of trailing brambles jostling with a jetsam of sticks, logs and the occasional football. By the turn of the new century, divested of death duties and supertax, the locals got together and cleaned it up. The result is river perfection near-as-damnit. An unruffled flow of water that divides striped lawns with small boathouses, on one bank, and river meadow on the other. Even the light here is different: leaf-filtered gentle nostalgia.

As children, we swam or canoed most of the backwaters here.

I remember my brother stealing my armbands when we swam across the river to look at the German E Boat they were using in the film *The Eagle Has Landed*. I had little choice, if I wanted to go home, but to grow a pair and swim back without them. Shortly after, he sat on piece of barbed wire in the river and had to go to hospital with a lacerated bottom for tetanus shots and stitches. Which was nice.

I've gone upmarket today in my little wooden boat that was built on the Broads during the 1930s. She found her way down south nearly fifty years ago, since when she has absorbed the Thames water into her very grain.

The Thames this afternoon is quiet before the storm, gearing up for Henley's Regatta in a couple of weeks and a steady stream of day trippers that goes from June to late September, when the last of any Indian summer trickles away along with the light.

It's worth remembering these waters weren't always so genteel.

Shrimp – for that is her name – has taken a similar journey to the Viking raiders who landed on the east coast and made their way up the Thames in long ships, all the way to Reading where they were forced to stop because the river narrowed and Alfred had finally woken up in a fighting mood. Pretty quickly, their leader, Gudrun, found Jesus.

During the English Civil War, the area was stoutly fought over – presumably because even Roundheads like messing about in boats.

Then Kenneth Grahame's imagination got a firm hold of it and populated the ancient woods – some of the oldest in the Kingdom – and grassy banks with Mole, Ratty and Toad and it finally assumed the role it was made for.

Lollygagging along.

I enter the backwater just after Unnamed Eyot[5] at the Wargrave end, almost lying flat to get under Fiddler's Bridge, which carries the quaint Willow Lane.

Allowing the current to do a good ninety percent of the work, I'm soon in my own world of glassy waters reflecting the clouds and sky. And silence.

Although not really, the willows and the water meadows with their tall grass and cowslip baffle the outside world in a way that allows one to tune into other sounds and senses. So, I stop rowing and let myself drift. Bees buzz, birds tattle and the wind does comb through the willows, on cue.

After about fifteen minutes of this, I tie up to a log, arrange cushions and pull out a book.

I wonder if Jerome K Jerome ever met Kenneth Graham and if they compared notes. In 1880 something he, Harris and George rowed up this backwater, stopped for lunch and nearly lost a meat pie. And Harris. Both George and JKJ agreed the pie was sorely missed.

I turn a few pages and find my spot.

Half-way up the backwater, we got out and lunched ... Harris had the beefsteak pie between his knees, and was carving it, and George and I were waiting with our plates ready.

"Have you got a spoon there?" says Harris;

"I want a spoon to help the gravy with."

The hamper was close behind us, and George and I both turned round to reach one out. We were not five seconds getting it. When we looked round again, Harris and the pie were gone!fIt was a wide, open field. There was not a tree or a bit of hedge for hundreds of yards. He could not have tumbled into the river, because we were on the water side of him, and he would have had to climb over us to do it. George and I gazed all about. Then we gazed at each other.

"Has he been snatched up to heaven?" I queried. "They'd hardly have taken the pie too," said George.

---

[5] The name for an island in the Thames, Saxon, I think. Spelled *Aight* (which is how it is pronounced) further downstream. London Saxons just have to be different.

There seemed weight in this objection, and we discarded the heavenly theory.

"I suppose the truth of the matter is," suggested George, descending to the commonplace and practicable, "that there has been an earthquake." And then he added, with a touch of sadness in his voice:

"I wish he hadn't been carving that pie." [6]

I didn't get much further but drifted off in the sun as the river, carrying thistledown but very little else, certainly not a soul, drifted past.

It had a definite bookish quality, my snooze today. From the moment I left the Thames thoroughfare, and turned the brass bow towards this infinite store of borrowed memory, it had felt like a narrative – in truth because I was looking for a literary ideal that afternoon: three friends (and a dog) expertly-captured in a bubble, moments of mirth and friendship away from the cares of a world that was soon to be on the march; of polite animals in their Sunday best; of passive indolence. But rivers do that, leaving dry land somehow makes things different: less real, yet more sane and safe. I snoozed and the cushion clouds above navigated their reflected way through the limpid waters and I dreamt of nothing much in a space that was timeless. Just a feeling of blameless rest, bobbing beside this lush first growth of buttercup and cowslip.

It felt polite.

I woke, satisfactorily, about twenty minutes later; feeling refreshed but feckless. So, I read some more, the pages of the book smelling warm and woody in the sun, pulled out a thermos for tea and a nearly-full packet of Jaffa cakes I'd filched from home earlier. Scoffed the lot, then rested my eyes some more.

Plonking people with mild insomnia on or by a river on a nice day is likely to work better than most prescription drugs. Fact.

---

[6] *Three Men in a Boat*, Jerome K Jerome

As the afternoon drew to a close, I untied and completed the rest of Hennerton's mile or so excursion from the main part of the River Thames, finishing with the near-perfect Johnson's Bridge, then a dog leg left onto the Thames above Marsh Lock.

The current was still brisk from the early spring flooding, so upstream was a bit of a slog. My penance for an indolent afternoon, but I didn't much mind – I needed the exercise and there was a pint waiting for me at the George and Dragon ... and my wife.

June

For the field is full of shades as I near a shadowy coast,
And a ghostly batsman plays to the bowling of a ghost,
And I look through my tears on a soundless-clapping host
As the run stealers flicker to and fro,
To and fro:
O my Hornby and my Barlow long ago!.

Francis Thompson

Place
Cricket Match.

Yes, but where, exactly?
Downside Abbey, Somerset.

Time of day
Who cares?

Conditions
Wry to wistful.

Drifting off pleasantly
Once I got a minute to myself.

Assisted by
Warm sun in my eyes and the gentle clock! of leather on willow.

Dreams?
Memories, more like.

Revelations?
Cricket could redeem us all.

Upon waking
Looked about energetically for signs of tea.

Overall rating
Civil.

FIELDNOTES

As the fusty end of the Nineteenth Century collided with the choppy start of the Twentieth, Cricket and the invention of the lightbulb conspired with one another to put an end to centuries of indolent catnapping.

Cricket had already been around for a long time.[7] About four hundred years, by most casual estimates. However, it didn't really get going outside of Kent and parts of London until English schoolboys came up with a set of rules everyone could more or less agree with,[8] who then went off after their A Levels and got jobs all over the British Empire, like a sort of expansionist Gap Year.

Now, this all roughly coincided with the incursion of the lightbulb in people's homes, which is relevant because it finally put biphasic sleep, quite literally, to bed. Suddenly you could do get on with things in the evening after it got dark, go to bed later and sleep through.

And, importantly for relevance to this book, both made a mess of the siesta, which explains the slightly bold statement at the start of this excursion.

Napping was no longer needed as people no longer got up at dawn, added to which Victorian Imperialists felt the siesta was

---

[7] Although not as long as the siesta.

[8] (in between doing the same for football and rugby)

rather too 'European' and altogether Catholic to be healthy for a Protestant Englishman who was getting used to the idea of running large parts of the planet. This meant a light lunch, a nice big tea and absolutely no letting up on healthy activities where your hands were visible at all times until gone 10pm. And this is where Cricket came in.

However, whilst Victorian inventiveness in general and Cricket specifically could be considered the enemy of loafing, it ignores one vital component to the game.

It's really boring.

And this is a gift to the ardent loafer-cum-spectator.

I've come back to the Old Place today as we've got kids who go here who I haven't seen in a while and, in the interests of multi-tasking, I've got until they've finished their matches to watch my match (Old Boys v Newer Boys).

Plus, it's got to be one of the nicest cricket pitches on the planet.

The people in charge of it have excelled themselves today. Vast, sloping lawns lead up from the Neogothic Abbey and its motley collection of almost-matching admin buildings, ante-diluvian classrooms, echoing halls and houses where The Houses are housed. The grass is a uniform 2cm until you get to the broad expanse that is the first team pitch and its sturdy Edwardian Pavilion.

Up here there's a nice view of the Abbey tower hovering above ancient beech trees and about fifteen billiard-flat acres of perfectly-chequered lawn.

There's also a white pergola where two very pretty ladies are serving Pimms.

I limit myself to a meagre five glasses, before tucking into a cold buffet lunch and catching up with people I like.

In keeping, I stop once in a while to watch play. That's the great thing about Cricket and one of the reasons I like it so much: in one very useful sense, anything above the fifty over format is made for people like me with a short attention span.

For prolonged periods, it's ample – and socially acceptable – to dip in and out, in between conversations, catching up on the news and stuffing your face. At most of the professional football matches I've been to, if you took out a newspaper, a pack of sandwiches and turned to your neighbour to chat about the weather and or the A303, you'd probably get punched in the face ... or, at the very least, told to leave.

We've nearly all got memories of playing on this pitch and that's another nice thing about being here.

I've got a good two hours until tea, so, after lunch, I take my leave and start out on a walk; down the tilting lawns, then (illegally) through the monk's private gardens, which have been taken over by rhododendrons the size of small clouds and wild onion as far as the eye can see. A wooded path takes me to where the monks used to have a swimming pool. It's been filled in but the delicately-carved wooden changing rooms that must have been built between the Wars are still there. I remember the pool when it was full of water and gulping carp.

The monks are now in exile and the place has a *Great Expectations* vibe, so my wandering describes a gentle arc, past the quiet Abbey and deserted monk's quarters, across a tussocky green that was once a croquet lawn and back to where the match ticks on in its timeless way.

I settle away from the crowds, by the boundary adjacent to square leg. The minute I lie down on the grass, I'm whisked back prep school aged about nine, pulling up tufts of grass, bored but too lazy to do anything about it. I'm old enough to remember boot whitener as a necessity. And shared boxes I'd rather not think about.

I watch the match for a bit, then take out a book.

It's one of those dozes that you're not aware at what point it actually started and real cricket became dream cricket. In any case one mirrored the other, in quite a satisfying way, because it was restful without being discombobulating. I dreamt of fielding, the smell of cut grass, a soothing breeze and a sort of calm contentment that this game and only this game can diffuse.

I woke, feeling supremely well-rested, I checked the time, then propped myself up on my elbow to watch the match and try and work out who was winning.

Instead, a movement caught my eye from lane leading up from the school. I turned, as my daughter appeared, still in her uniform, which includes a tartan skirt that could stop a bullet. She was grinning as she spotted me from a distance, walking alongside her elder brother who was managing to look simultaneously scruffy and well-turned-out.

And I felt my heart give a squeeze.

July

The unwise man
is awake all night
worries over and again.
When morning rises
he is restless still,
his burden as before..

Hávamál (Viking book of wisdom)

Place
Holy Island

Yes, but where, exactly?
Adjacent to the both geometrically and aesthetically pleasing slopes of Lindisfarne Castle.

Time of day
Midday

Conditions
Hot, going on testy.

Drifting off pleasantly
Challenging due to the scourge of tourism.

Assisted by
Reading up on the scourge of Vikings.

Dreams?
Scant

Revelations?
No-one can resist an island, especially one with a causeway.

Upon waking
Discovered a raging thirst for cold lager. Preferably Danish.

Overall rating
Scorcher!

FieldNotes

The life of an author is sometimes that of the wandering bard ... or wayfaring itinerant, depending on which side of bed you get out on. One week a school in Bracknell, the next a library in Stoke ... a reading in a bookshop somewhere off the M5. All the while surviving solely off one's wits and service station mini scotch eggs. A car whose central console storage is a thicket of own brand chocolate wrappers and defunct phone chargers is the price we pay for our art.

This week it's Redcar, the home both of the first ever lifeboat on the planet and 2015 Third Place in Britain's Ugliest New Building Competition, aka the Carbuncle Cup.

A quick whizz round town to gawp at said boat and damnable carbuncle after my authoring duties (diligently over exciting nine-year-olds) and then I'm off.

Lindisfarne, the Holy Island, is my destination, via Durham to pick up my wife and our dog. Of the two, Cooper is the most pleased to see me – by some margin. Hélène was enjoying the Newcastle Retail Experience and she's looked up Lindisfarne and suspects I'm taking her to see folk music.

Assurances, as we slingshot the Newcastle ring road system, that there really are two Lindisfarnes are met with narrow-eyed skepticism. They are both very ancient, I admit – but one definitely worth paying a visit to, after we've stayed the night with friends over the border in Scotland. And it won't involve singing along to 'Fog on the Tyne' in a not-very-crowded pub. There will be views. H likes views.

The next day we get up to glorious sunshine on Scottish hills and much more positive mental attitudes all round.

Helped on our way by our friend producing a hearty cooked breakfast including soft-boiled eggs with little wooly hats on, we get in the car and loop the slender neck of Britannia until the undomesticated Northumberland coast opens up before us like a triptych in landscape.

It takes a bit of trial and error before we find the causeway and then we're off! Describing a broad arc, which I can't be bothered to describe, we come to one of those giant carparks that you usually find at ski resorts or outside mega shopping centres with a bowling alley attached.

Cooper leaps out of the back of the car as if he's been waiting his whole life for this and immediately looks for something edible (bits of sandwich, ice cream, preferably, goose poo comes a close second), then pees on a sun-warmed tyre.

H does none of these things, but does make a note of the time that the causeway shuts as I go to the ticket machine, prod buttons and wave my card at it in a hopeful way.

We've got a good four hours. Mindful of The Woman in Black and what happens to southern folk who get cut off from the outside world, I make a mental note to stay three hours, tops, as we set out towards the village in staggered file with other day trippers.

I love English seaside towns, and this is a great example, with an extra 37% history thrown in. It's got all the stuff a proper community needs: Primary School, an Express Supermarket, a library and at least a couple of 'proper' shops selling things like haircuts or normal shoes, plus tasteful tourist outlets and a ruddy great Abbey (in pieces, scattered over attractive green turf).

Honestly, you can easily see why the Vikings were attracted to it.

First stop after a stand selling quite delicious honeycomb, is the 7th century St Mary the Virgin Church (as opposed to the other Saint Mary who was almost certainly not a virgin). It's worth it just for the fact it's the oldest maintained building on the Island.

Before it became a Victorian Daguerreotype, then Instagram hit, Lindisfarne was predominantly all about Saints. The easy ones are St Aidan and St Cuthbert, but then there's saints Fianan, Colmàn, Balin, Tuda, Eadberht, Eadfrith, and Aethelwold. That's a lot of beatification for a not-even-proper island, but even with daytrippers from Edinburgh and Newcastle milling about with strawberry mivvie's in their hands, it still feels special. There's a vibe.

Before the tourists came, when it was all broad skies and screeching gulls, to fill the time, they put quill to vellum. The most notable example is the Lindisfarne Gospels, apparently down to their Celtic, Germanic and Roman fusion illuminations and the first bits of the Gospel in English anywhere.

Viking raids put a stop to most of that in the 8th century. 793 was a pretty shit year for Lindisfarne, especially if you were a monk. The Anglo-Saxon Chronicle records not only large hairy men with axes but

'...excessive whirlwinds, lightning, and fiery dragons in the sky...'

However, then all that went away and things were pretty good for about the next eight hundred years. Until another thug with a big beard, in the form of Henry VIII, came along, bashed the place about and – ever one to make a statement – built a castle. And this edifice more or less defined the image of Holy Island, ironically now it was substantially less holy, and essentially a military instillation.

We take a lot of pictures, as we make our way towards the castle. It's so iconic a view from the middle distance, rather like the

Eiffel Tower or the Pyramids, that you're half-expecting it to be a disappointment. But it isn't. The castle seems fused with the land, twisting out of the rock at just the perfect point on the horizon to look imposing without imposing itself too much on the natural landscape. Lutyens then did a good job civilising the place in the early 1900s.

It starts to feel quite bucket and spade, as a long beach curls off in the direction of Scotland. To the south, Bamber lurks in the distance, like a violent older brother.

It's rather busy and I'm just beginning to wonder if I'm going to need to forcibly corkscrew my head into the sand in order to get a decent forty winks when we suddenly come across a lovely and quite unexpected garden, walled off from the elements ... and quiet. H, spends a good fifteen minutes critiquing the borders, then takes the hint and leaves me.

I plonk myself on a bench amongst a storm of lobelia and attempt to snooze, but with difficulty. It's more of a resting eye affair because there's a steady stream of people who feel the need to look at the garden – because it's there. They all do the same thing, namely walk in, stand right by my bench and announce, 'it's a garden!' to their companions who all reply, 'Yes, it is!'

Unreasonably annoyed by this, I keep my eyes tight shut and do manage two or three interludes where my mind drifts, bobbing along the sandy shallows of swoon.

It's OK, and probably all I need as I had a massive lie in and have done bugger all today except potter about.

I stretch, abruptly aware that I've got a raging thirst for very cold lager, get up and go in search of H and the dog.

August

*I don't think necessity is the mother of invention.
Invention, in my opinion, arises directly from idleness,
possibly also from laziness – to save oneself trouble..*

Agatha Christie, somewhere or other

Place
Achmelvich Bay.

Yes, but where, exactly?
Near Ullapool, W Scotland.

Time of day
All of it.

Conditions
Positively mediatic, unless you go in the water.

Drifting off pleasantly
Oh, several times.

Assisted by
Lots of healthy outdoor activities.

Dreams?
Spartan.

Revelations?
This could be the future of bucket and spade holidays.

Upon waking
Grappled with sand.

Overall rating
Bracing.

FIELDNOTES

If you look up 'Ullapool' online the top result is 'What to do in Ullapool when it rains'.

According to experts, hand-picked for being able to count beyond twenty or thirty, it fair buckets down for well over half the year up here and for most of the other days the Met Office describes the overall conditions as being either 'cloudy', 'mostly cloudy' or 'overcast'.

Now you might suspect that this tells you all you need to know about Northwest Scotland in general, and Ullapool, specifically. Except it doesn't.

Because this leaves the nimble visitor about five days a year of glorious sunshine, unfiltered by Stratus, and untotally ruined by sheets of freezing rain. It is during this brief window that the beaches of north by northwest of Glasgow are a paradise on Earth and you'd do well to stop what you are doing elsewhere in the British Isles and go there immediately.

Near-white sand beaches can be found here, scalloped by tide and time into compact bays, fringed with heather and the sort of grass you see in expensive gardens that tends to look spikey. The sea changes with the light in a way that normally only happens in the Adriatic or doctored postcards. It starts the day pale jade, grading to china blue, then lapis lazuli ... small waves supplying the white marbling, before it wraps things up in pensive ultramarine.

I pick Achmelvich Bay because I think I've been here before, about ten years ago, with friends and masses of our small children.

We went to Ullapool, at any rate, when we were callow and unaware of its beachy charms and the fact it is the home of the science of plate tectonics and once-bastion of the herring industry (with some limply flapping mackerel tossed in).

We did do a bit of fishing that time, but we mainly tramped across miles of heather looking for wildlife that wasn't there. Then we went to the beach.

If we didn't go to this one, then it was one very like it, I think, as I park the car and crest the hill.

It's hot – well, quite warm, almost balmy – and I've driven all the way in *crocs* and shorts. You know, to get into the mood. I've only come from as far afield as Fort William today (two hours, tops) but I'm itching to get down to the sea and sandy stuff.

As I get around the corner, I wonder if it's closed or there's been a zombie apocalypse overnight, as there's not a soul there. True, I did see a few cars and the odd lorry on my way up, but they could have been fleeing.

Still, it is only 7.30 am on a Tuesday and the seaside is as good a place as any to escape the undead, who I'm minded to think stick to urban areas and are probably terrible swimmers, anyway.

When it comes to sleep, Scotland is potentially a tricky part of the world. Too much dark in the winter, for starters. Lights out just gone 3pm in the run up to Christmas, which gives you almost no time for honest daylight hour snoozing in between, not that you probably need it. And almost endless days in the summer: Shetland gets nineteen hours during the Solstice, so a reversion to 'student hours' is the only option i.e. going to bed at 3am, when it finally gets dark and sleeping until lunch or until

Prisoner Cell Block H comes on. Like so much else up here, life is a gritty challenge for the committed northern loafer.

My Granny, who was from these parts and could tend towards the zealous herself, liked to say that a man needs seven hours sleep, a woman eight and a fool, nine. As she tucked into her neat scotch and clootie dumpling.

I'm not sure how lazing around on a beach on a school day is viewed, but there has been some revisionism of late. The odd *Hurkle Durkle* (Scottish for Duvet Day in their tradition of reducing everything to glottal stops) is supposed to reduce one's chance of a heart attack by 63%. It's a suspiciously precise figure but would be well worth it even if we're talking 2%, frankly.

I'm knackered after yesterday's drive, compounded with last night's never-quite-the-same-as-home hotel bed and I begin to feel my eyes closing. I'm tempted to give in to it, but don't want to peak too soon, so I prop myself up on an elbow and look about instead, as the place is becoming almost lively.

Most of my fellow beach occupants seem to be of the serious sporting variety: there's now a lot of kit cluttering up the beach designed to help people slide over the surface of the water with the help of wind and waves and I'm beginning to wish I bought a wetsuit – you know, to fit in.

The sand and the sea look straight out of a brochure – so that's all good and totally what I was hoping for when I decided to come all this way. The former is flour-white, flat as a clean sheet where it joins the latter's jolly bands of blue and green, like an aquatic tie die.

I notice someone small has stopped to consider me. He's about four, I'd say and, apart from a runny nose that doesn't seem to trouble him a jot, he's remarkable for the fact that his shorts would probably fit me. He could be wearing them comfortably into the next decade.

He's giving the dog a look that is in equal part fear and yearning.

'Cooper,' I jiggle the dog's lead to get his attention and look around for the boy's mother. 'He's very friendly!' I sort of project over to the best candidate for the job, who is watching us from about fifteen yards away.

'My wee boy or your wee dog?' asks the mum in that lowland Scottish accent that ranks alongside Geordie and Southern Irish for *Most Attractive Regional Accent in the English Language* the world over.

My own company for the last fourteen hours has dulled my wits. 'Ha!' is pretty much all I can think of saying and suck in my stomach ... because I'm incredibly shallow. I turn to the boy. 'You can stroke him, if you like ...' whilst looking over at the mum, in case I've misread the situation, but she smiles.

'Go on Guy, the nice doggie won't bite you ...' she gives me a stagey grin, '... we don't think.'

On the basis that small children have a tendency to drop food and don't mind their fingers being licked, Cooper is well up for the job. Perhaps a bit enthusiastic, because the wee guy, wee Guy, takes a couple of panicky steps back and sort of pats the air about a foot above the dog's head.

'Don't be such a wuss,' the mum says and I definitely decide I like her.

'Look,' I say to Guy and pat Cooper's head and then his back to make him sit. 'Just like this.'

Dog and boy, both with about the same mental age briefly bond to the exclusion of all else ... and then the moment is over. He goes back to his mother and I sit down to go back to my solitary tourism.

Then I hear a metallic clink, which makes me look up again.

'Would you like a cup of tea?' She's got a proper thermos and everything.

'Fantastic,' I say.

'That's good, I've made about a gallon of this stuff and there's nowhere to pee for miles.'

A decent interval after Elevenses, I reckon it's warm enough to go for a swim.

Sixteen seconds into the water, I realise why everyone else has a wetsuit.

The North Atlantic doesn't get much more northern than this. The outside air temperature might be August but it's still November in the water.

Guy, who is 'looking after' Cooper waves at me and I wave back a bit too manically before striking out to sea in a noisy crawl that I hope covers the sound of my whimpering.

I warm up eventually, enough to slow down to a more leisurely breaststroke the better to appreciate the fact the sea is crystal clear and the bottom is dotted with small clumps of seaweed, like they've been carefully planted on the seabed. I've got my prescription goggles, so I spend my five minutes before my brain shuts down and my heart eventually stops peering at these clumps of green against the white sand and the occasional crustacean toiling along.

'You look cold,' says Guy's mum.

'I am,' I admit. 'Do I have icicles hanging off my eyebrows?'

'There's more tea?'

'Thanks, but I think I should keep moving and the dog needs a walk.'

We get back in time for Guy and Cooper to exchange heartfelt goodbyes, then both become instantly distracted by something else (Guy, the prospect of an icecream, Cooper a seagull). And I plonk myself back down on the sand, feeling perfectly warm again.

I've bought ham and cheese sandwiches, which I share with Cooper and a melted Twix, which I don't; then I make a sort of sand pillow for myself, rearrange my towel and pull out my book.

When I wake up, I genuinely can't remember where I am for the first eight to ten seconds.

If I'd woken up to dragons scorching tunnels of flame across the sky, an oncoming train or a leafy glade full nymphs playing harps, it would have been no less bewildering. I must have been out for under fifteen minutes, judging by the fact the sun has hardly moved, but the sleep was dreamless and profound. And a little unnerving.

My brain makes a beeline for the mundane and I check on Cooper who is hogging most of the shade from the miniature beech umbrella I had the presence of mind to throw in the car at the last minute. Then I turn on my side and go back to my book.

And so passes the rest of the day as I unwind exquisitely. I read after an intermittent fashion, the dog sees to his feet, we both snooze, half in and half out of a sun which climbs to the sky's apex and seems to hover there until teatime, when it eventually starts to lose its heat and sink towards the hills.

We go for another walk and I buy myself a garish ice cream that looks like an LGBT rocket ship.

The tide seems to have barely shifted all day and so I take another paddle – for form's sake – before packing up my few things and going back to the car.

September

You haven't really been anywhere until you've got back home.
Terry Pratchett, *The Light Fantastic*

Place
Chez Bennett.

Yes, but where, exactly?
Living Room sofa, next to a slightly unnecessary fire and gently snoring dog.

Time of day
Betwixt lunch and a bracing walk.

Conditions
Just so.

Drifting off pleasantly
Barely got through the first page of the Sunday Times Sports Section.

Assisted by
Blood-curdling threats to offspring.

Dreams?
Just thoughts, really.

Revelations?
Thankfully none.

Upon waking
Talked to dog.

Overall rating
The absolute best.

FIELDNOTES

Sunday mornings are for doing something physical. And I don't necessarily mean clogging up the B roads of Great Britain with other men dressed in Lycra. Although I enjoy cycling when I get around to it, it generally only happens when I'm trying to get somewhere in a hurry and there isn't a car, taxi or a horse at hand.

If I'm not being dragged to church, I prefer doing something practical with my Sunday morning, like chopping up large lumps of wood to make them into slightly smaller lumps of wood, digging pointlessly ... or, better still, something mildly dangerous up a tree or on a roof. With power tools. Anything that gets the blood up, really. And I do realise that would have got me into ecclesiastic trouble back in the day, but I'm going for the *mens sana in corpore sano* defence.

Then, showered and coiffed, I like to collar one of the kids and beat them soundly at pool or table tennis – two of a dwindling list of things at which I'm still marginally better at than them. We snaffle cold beer from the fridge on our way out to the barn: to help get my eye in, for me; low level bribery, for them. They get to choose the playlist.

Sunday lunch is the crowning achievement of Western Civilisation. This is a considered opinion, based on cold, objective fact.

Sunday lunch combines all our best ingredients. Volume eating of garden produce, we generally save our best cuts of meat for Sunday, ditto claret and a broad range of well-chosen auxiliary drinks, combined with healthy family time, and permission to then loaf about – sanctioned by God. Plus there's gravy.

After triumphing at pool, I'll leave my sobbing offspring to their grief and shame and saunter into the kitchen to mix my wife a stiff gin and raid the larder for nibbles.

Drawn to the smell of salty snacks, the kids/dog/guests will gravitate towards the kitchen to eat Frazzles (or olives, if we're feeling upmarket) whilst crispy, bloody things get carved and the table gets laid. I think it's important to make an occasion of these events, so out will come whatever is left of the wedding tableware that hasn't been broken or lost and I'll put on a clean shirt and, very possibly, wash my hands.

Wine should be as costly as thine habit can afford, to paraphrase Polonius into what he really meant to say. And decanted. Anyone half-civilised should always have a half bottle of decent pudding wine in the fridge at any one time.

About an hour later, begat of about two pounds of red meat, several glasses of claret and a litre of custard, it's time to put on marigolds, fill the sink with near to boiling water and hit the pots and pans with gusto (vim and vigour, not Spanish sidekick).

Once the herculean task of degreasing and de-potatoeing trays and saucepans is completed, I'll pour myself a generous measure of Armagnac, grab my coffee, any chocolate on offer and make myself scarce.

Turning on the television in the living room is a snooze-beginner's error, as it only attracts attention, so stealth it must be: Sunday papers and dog. Cooper is here partly for the narrative aesthetics, partly because with him dribbling by my side I'm not going to wake up to an empty house, whilst everyone has pissed off for a nice Sunday Walk. Cooper seems to have a very reliable timer in what is otherwise a fairly empty head that says *Walkies!* is precisely nineteen minutes after the washing up is done.

Sleeping in exotic places is all very well, but there's nothing quite like forty winks at home for seamless slumber. The fire crackles, the clock ticks, the dog exhales ... and the mind drifts between its well-earned rest and the relaxing sounds of the familiar.

The right to rest is undeniable and universal: every living thing does it – far better than humans for the most part. Cows are especially good at coasting through life, but we've also built it into our machines, most of which have a rest mode, which we humans seem to approve of. Deep sleep is an essential (lest we go mad and expire), but I'd argue that sloth is, too. Shutting down for brief periods is to reflect but without thought, to inhabit an adjacent reality for a brief period, to wake with an altered take on life that, at the very least, reminds us it's not all a headlong rush.

Sunday napping is the pinnacle, I feel. It's the perfect end to a week and a fitting end to this little book which I dedicate to the gentle art of indolence and to my family for allowing me to pursue it ... in a sort of feckless way.

THE END ...

zzzzzzzzzz...

When Robin grew up, he thought he wanted to be a soldier until everyone else realised that putting him in charge of a tank was a very bad idea. He then became an assistant gravedigger, a private tutor to the rich and famous, entrepreneur ... until finally settling down to write improbable stories to stop his children killing each other on long car journeys. He once heard himself described on the radio travel news as 'some twit' when his car broke down and blocked the rush hour traffic around Marble Arch. This is about right. Robin is married with three children, one of whom illustrated this book. He spends his time between France and England.

@writer_robin

Jude spent most of his formative years in the south of France where it was uncertain that years of inattentive doodling in lessons would come to any use. However, when he was asked to illustrate his second book, a degree in modern languages was beginning to seem a less profitable enterprise by comparison. When not on a muddy building site, Jude enjoys many ordinary things like playing the guitar, rugby and walking his dog along the river. Although he grew up in France, he now spends his days in Bristol where he studies and where the earnings of this book will be spent in its finest drinking establishments.

For more books by
Robin Bennett

visit

www.robinbennett.net

or catch up with him on social media

@writer_robin

For talks or enquiries email

press@monsterbooks.co.uk

MONSTER BOOKS

also by
Robin Bennett:

Fieldsports, Foraging and Terrible Ordeals

Illustrations *by* Jude Bennett

MONSTER BOOKS

January
IN WHICH A GOOSE IS COOKED

When I was about seven years old, my father woke one morning and told us, in all seriousness, that not another day could go by without him tasting the sweet flesh of a goose.

He packed me, our cairn terrier, Judy, and his shotgun into our rusting Morris Marina and strapped a canoe onto the roof rack. Then he set off for the river.

I had my doubts even at the early stages of this enterprise: it was January and freezing cold. On top of this, my father had never expressed a craving for goose before, so I felt pretty sure it would soon pass if the call was left unanswered. However, at seven years old, you just kind of go along with things – especially if your father is anything like mine.

We arrived at a bleak stretch of the Thames somewhere near Reading and prepared everything whilst watching the flock of Canada geese lounging about on an island in the middle of the river. Then we got in the canoe: me at the front with the dog; my father at the back, armed to the teeth.

The few walkers who were braving the weather that morning jumped in the air and looked about in alarm as the first shot rang out. Only the goose my father had picked for his dinner seemed unperturbed, as the pellets simply bounced off the thick mattress of breast feathers from twenty yards away.

Undeterred and completely unaware of the sharp looks he was getting from the bank, my father reloaded and paddled closer.

When the second shot rang out, taking the unfortunate goose's head off, people really stopped to stare.

Several things happened rather quickly after that:

My father (still armed) jumped out of the canoe, retrieved a limply flapping goose and threw it on my lap; he then jumped back in, sliding the shotgun down the side of the canoe; whereupon the shotgun's second barrel went off, with a sort of muffled bang; *and we started to sink*. My father panicked: he threw me onto the bank of the island, along with the dog; paddled as fast as he could across the river in a leaking boat; jumped out of the canoe with the shotgun in one hand, the dead goose in the other; and scampered towards the car.

Then he drove off.

It had been an eventful few minutes, but the next part of the morning went very slowly indeed as I stood on that cold island with the dog and wondered what would happen next.

Eventually a put-upon-looking lockkeeper appeared on the opposite bank, got into a small motor launch and made his way across to where I stood. He picked me up, muttering something about a phone call, and took me back to shore to meet my father – who'd had time to go home, wash the blood off and hide the goose.

Two weeks later, we would be sitting in front of the TV with trays on our laps watching Tom Baker being Doctor Who and stuffing our faces with goose. The whole operation was pronounced a great success.